CLOSER LOOK AT

MOUNTAINS

Cally Hall

COPPER BEECH BOOKS
Brookfield, Connecticut

© Aladdin Books Ltd 1999
Designed and produced by
Aladdin Books Ltd
28 Percy Street
London W1P 0LD

*First published in the United States
in 1999 by*
Copper Beech Books,
an imprint of
The Millbrook Press
2 Old New Milford Road
Brookfield, Connecticut 06804

Editor
Michael Flaherty

Designer
Gary Edgar-Hyde

Picture Research
Brooks Krikler Research

Front cover illustration
Gary Edgar-Hyde

Illustrators
Gary Edgar-Hyde, Mike Saunders, Peter Kesteven,
Stephen Sweet — Simon Girling and Associates,
Ian Moores, Rob Shone

Consultant
Joyce Pope

Certain illustrations have appeared in
earlier books created by Aladdin Books.

Printed in Belgium
Cataloging-in-Publication Data is on file at the
Library of Congress.

ISBN 0-7613-0902-0 (lib. bdg.)

5 4 3 2 1

CONTENTS

INTRODUCTION

Mountains are the highest places on earth. Whether as single peaks or part of mountain chains, they provide some of the most spectacular views in the world. To some, they may seem peaceful havens, but they are also hazardous. Avalanches, volcanic eruptions, and earthquakes occur in mountainous areas, often as a result of mountain-building processes. Mountains provide great resources, but they are also barriers to transportation and trade, to animals and plants, and even weather.

Isolated peak
The symmetrical cone of a volcano forms this isolated peak. Its sides have been built by a series of layers of ash and lava that have erupted from the volcano.

From the highest mountains to the deepest valleys, our earth is a world of contrasts. There are mountains on the continents and beneath the oceans. Chains of mountains and isolated peaks rise from the seafloor, taller even than the highest mountains on land. Immense forces have been at work to raise such enormous masses of solid rock.

MOUNTAINS

ANDES

The Andes is the longest mountain system in the world, with mountains on land and under the sea. Its mountain ranges cover a distance of about 5,500 miles (8,900 kilometers) along the west side of South America, and continue southward under the sea. In the sixteenth century, the Spanish conquistadors called this mountain system a cordillera, meaning "rope."

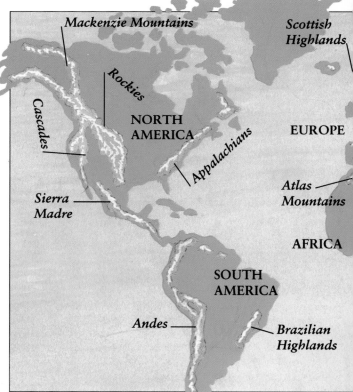

The map above shows the major mountain systems of the world. Early maps were improved as explorers traveled farther afield. Satellite images from space now help us map the

ON CLOSER INSPECTION
– *Midatlantic Ridge*

The Midatlantic Ridge runs like a spine down the middle of the Atlantic Ocean, a distance of about 7,000 miles (11,300 km). It is a zone of volcanic activity, which can be seen where it rises above the surface of the sea in Iceland and Ascension Island.

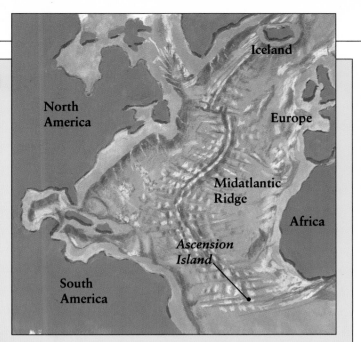

OF THE EARTH

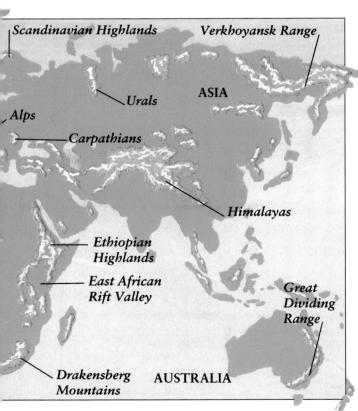

ALPS

The highest mountains in Europe, the Alps extend in an arc cutting through seven countries like a jagged spine, about 750 miles (1,200 kilometers) long. They form a climatic barrier, shielding some of the warm Mediterranean countries from the cold of northern Europe. The sources of the Rhine, Rhône, and Danube rivers begin in the Alps.

mountain regions on land. Sonar (sound) equipment on ships show that there is a system of submarine (underwater) mountains in the ocean (*see* On Closer Inspection, above).

Sugar Loaf Mountain

The summit of Rio de Janeiro's Sugar Loaf Mountain, in Brazil, towers 1,296 feet (395 m) over Guanabara Bay. The mountain is a rock dome formed when magma (molten rock) pushed upward from beneath the surface. The magma cooled and solidified before reaching the surface. Wearing away (erosion) of the overlying rock has exposed the solid granite below.

The world's surface is made up of enormous pieces. The pieces are called tectonic plates. They are not fixed in place, but very slowly move about. When they pull apart, chains of volcanoes are formed. In some places they push into each other. As a result, mountains are forced up, often at the edges of continents.

HOW MOUNT

THE HIMALAYAS

The highest mountain system on land is the Himalayas. It was named Himalaya from the Sanskrit, meaning "abode of the snow." Rocks of the Himalayas once formed the bed of an ancient ocean, called the Tethys. The mountains began to form about thirty-eight million years ago as the ocean closed, and India and Asia collided. The land at the edges of the continents was crumpled and pushed upward to form mountains. The Himalayas are still rising as India continues to push northward.

The diagram (left) shows the position of India in relation to Asia about fifty million years ago. The blue lines show the boundaries between the plates that make up the earth's crust. The red arrows show the direction that the continents are being carried on their plates. The plate carrying India is moving faster than that of Asia.

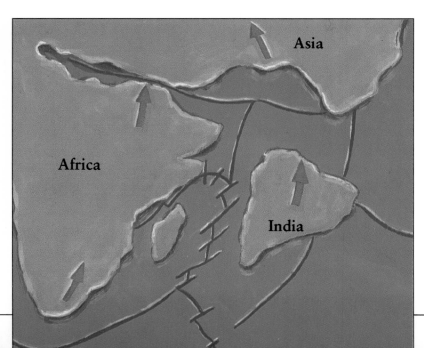

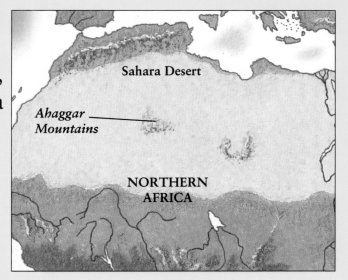

AINS ARE FORMED

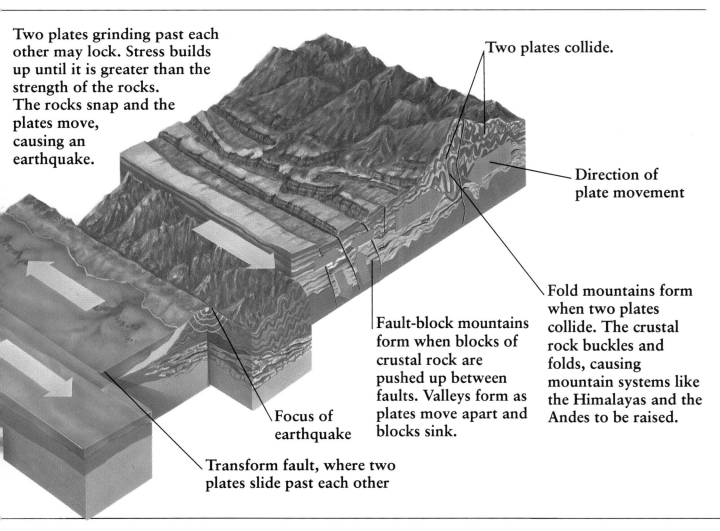

Two plates grinding past each other may lock. Stress builds up until it is greater than the strength of the rocks. The rocks snap and the plates move, causing an earthquake.

Two plates collide.

Direction of plate movement

Fold mountains form when two plates collide. The crustal rock buckles and folds, causing mountain systems like the Himalayas and the Andes to be raised.

Fault-block mountains form when blocks of crustal rock are pushed up between faults. Valleys form as plates move apart and blocks sink.

Focus of earthquake

Transform fault, where two plates slide past each other

Grand Teton

The mountains of Grand Teton National Park, in the Rockies (below), are fault-block mountains. The rocks are 2.5 billion years old, but the mountains only

s rock is squeezed, it can crumple and form fold mountains. Too much pressure too quickly causes the rock to fault, or fracture, into great blocks. Mountains may form as these blocks of rock are tilted or lifted up. Forces below the crust can cause it to bulge upward to form domes.

FOLDS AND

started to form about ten million years ago when a fault (crack) appeared in the crust. There were earthquakes, as the rocks on either side of the fault shifted. As the block west of the fault was uplifted to form the mountains, the block to the east dropped to form the floor of the valley known as Jackson Hole. The Teton Range rises abruptly, in places towering more than 6,600 feet (2,000 m) from the valley floor.

DOMES

Dome mountains have folds that dip away in every direction from a central area. They form when magma below the crust collects in a cavity. Pressure builds up as more magma collects. Rock layers above are pushed upward, forming a huge, rounded bump.

A dome mountain is formed as pressure below lifts the crust to form an upfold.

Rocks may fracture when they are either pulled apart or compressed. As tectonic plates move, enormous fault blocks are forced up or down (left) to form new mountains and valleys.

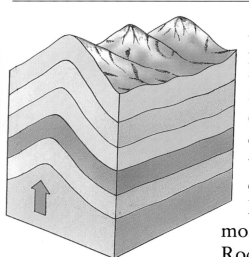

Block sinks, forming a valley.

Block rises, forming mountains.

– *Black smokers*

In 1977, scientists found large colonies of strange animals surviving in hot, mineral-rich water gushing up from cracks in the seabed. These hydrothermal vents are mainly found near underwater volcanoes along spreading midoceanic ridges, such as the Midatlantic Ridge. The communities include giant tube worms more than 10 feet (3 m) long.

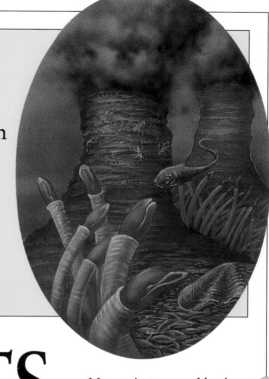

AND PLANTS

Mountain trees and bushes have hard, woody roots that can hold fast in cracks in the rocks and in thin soil.

MOUNTAIN

VEGETATION ZONES
As the altitude increases and temperature falls, the type of vegetation changes. These zones of vegetation support different sorts of animals.

The deciduous forests below the Alps give way to coniferous forest in the foothills. Higher up on grassy slopes, alpine plants and low-lying shrubs survive. Beneath the snow line, only a few lichens and mosses cling to rocks.

The rain forest of East Africa gives way to bamboo in the foothills. Higher up the slope are heath and moorland, and above these, the African equivalent of the alpine zone, with low grasses and low, dense plants.

Apollo butterfly

Snow line

Lichen

Condor

Edelweiss

Mountain hare

Monkey puzzle tree

Alpine tundra

Grizzly bear

Bighorn sheep

Conifers and shrubs

Puma

Bamboo

Gorilla

Temperate forest

Bromeliad

Elephant

Tropical forest

Tapir

Life for people in the mountains is not easy. Thin soil, low rainfall, and low temperatures make farming difficult. Mountain people rely heavily on hardy mountain animals they have domesticated. These animals are a vital source of food and clothing, and ma be the only source of transportation.

MOUNTAIN

Machu Picchu
This fortress city was built by native American Indians called Incas. It is built on a series of terraces cut into the side of a mountain in the Andes, more than 7,480 feet (2,280 m) above sea level. The city covers an area of five square miles (13 square kilometers).

Portable oxygen
At high altitudes the air becomes thin, so climbers carry oxygen in pressurized tanks. They breathe it through a tube and face mask.

MOUNTAIN PEOPLE AND THEIR LIVESTOCK
Mountain people, such as the Bhotia of the Himalayas, have adapted physically to the thin mountain air; they have larger lungs and blood richer in oxygen-carrying red blood cells. They depend on the yak (below) for transportation, meat, wool, and butter. Native people of the Andes show the same physical adaptations and depend on the llama in much the same way.

ON CLOSER INSPECTION
– *Traders with camels*

Sturdy, two-humped Bactrian camels carry heavy loads for traders who cross mountain routes and travel through deserts. Camels traveled the Silk Road (100 B.C.–A.D. 1650) taking traders to collect silk from the East to trade in the West.

PEOPLES

TIBETAN MONASTERIES

Monasteries high in the mountains of Tibet provide peace and solitude for Buddhist monks (below). Most people find it difficult to breathe at altitudes above about 9,850 feet (3,000 m), but the monks have become used to the thin air. Their capital, Lhasa, lies 12,000 feet (3,600 m) above sea level. Rising a further 330 feet (110 m) above Lhasa is the Potala, a golden-roofed palace that was a former residence of the Dalai Lama.

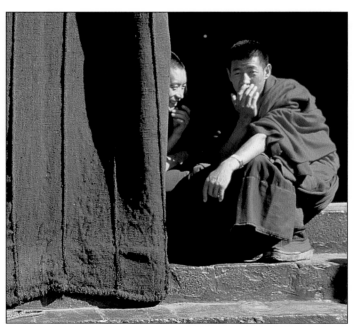

CONTOUR FARMING

Mountain people are expert at farming as much land as possible. They build terraces along the steep mountainsides, following the contours. Mountain streams are diverted to irrigate the system of terraced fields (above).

Many mountains contain valuable resources such as metal ores and gemstones. Vast areas are mined for the minerals they contain. Mountain forests are felled to provide wood. Mountain habitats are changed or destroyed when such resources are mined or harvested.

MOUNTAIN

Reservoir

Dams are built across mountain valleys to make large artificial lakes called reservoirs (above). Reservoirs provide water for homes, industry, and farming. But the flooding of valleys devastates the local wildlife.

GEYSERS

Geysers (left) are underground springs that throw columns of boiling water and steam into the air at intervals. Hot magma (molten rock) beneath the surface heats underground water. This hot water and steam can be used to spin turbines to generate electricity in hydrothermal (hot water) power plants. In some places in Iceland, the water is pumped directly into homes and greenhouses to heat them. Water can be pumped underground so that it is heated by the molten rock before it is used in power plants. Regions with many volcanoes, such as New Zealand, Japan, and Iceland, make use of the heat from underground molten rock to generate electricity in power plants. More than 40 percent of Iceland's electricity is generated in this way.

ON CLOSER INSPECTION
– *Mountain forests*

Destruction of mountain forests for timber, as in Indonesia and Thailand, leaves the land bare. The rain then washes the soil downhill. Rivers become clogged with the soil, causing flooding.

RESOURCES

Hydroelectricity
Many parts of the world get electricity from hydroelectric (water-driven) power plants (below). Water is channeled from natural or artificial mountain lakes down through pipes or tunnels to the power plants. As the water travels downhill it gains speed. The force of the water as it arrives at the power plant spins turbines that drive generators that produce electricity.

MINING IN THE MOUNTAINS

Many of the world's largest copper mines (above) are in mountains. Chile is one of the main producers of copper. The world's highest mine is a sulfur mine in Chile at an altitude of 19,700 feet (6,000 m) on the Aucanquilcha volcano. Bolivian and Chilean miners, who have adapted to the altitude, help work this dangerous mine.

The main income of many mountain regions is from tourism. Walking, climbing, and skiing attract many vacationers, as do fishing, rock climbing, and hang gliding. National parks, trails, and walkways have been introduced to lessen the damage to the landscape and wildlife brought about by our desire to visit mountain regions.

MOUNTAIN

Mountain climbing

Mountain climbing is a popular sport. For safety, people usually climb with a partner or in a small group. It is essential to have warm clothing and the right equipment. The weather can change rapidly, turning a simple climb into a formidable challenge.

Snowboarding

Snowboarding is a fairly new sport that is becoming more and more popular. This exciting sport was designated a new Olympic sport at the 1998 Winter Olympics in Japan.

THE ALPS AND SKI RESORTS

The Alps stretch over 750 miles (1,200 km). Thousands of tourists travel there each year to enjoy the clean air and spectacular scenery, to ski, climb, and hike. The area of the Alps shown below is a very popular ski region.

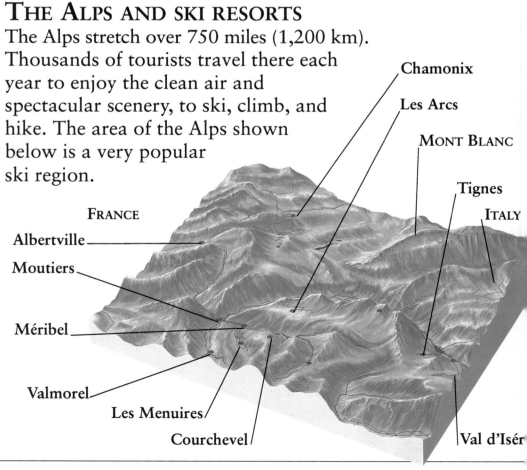

FRANCE

Chamonix
Les Arcs
MONT BLANC
Tignes
ITALY

Albertville
Moutiers
Méribel
Valmorel
Les Menuires
Courchevel
Val d'Isér

ON CLOSER INSPECTION
– Ascent of Everest, 1953

The summit of the world's highest mountain, Mount Everest, was finally reached by Sir Edmund Hillary of New Zealand and Tenzing Norgay of Nepal on May 29, 1953. They carried food and equipment, including an oxygen supply. They belonged to a British expedition led by Sir John Hunt.

RECREATION

Hiking

For those not athletic enough for the higher slopes, hiking (below) can give enormous pleasure. Well-loved and regularly walked routes are now often protected by paved trails. Many walkers damage the countryside if such footpaths are not laid. Bicycle routes and trails for horseback riding are also marked in some parks.

HANG GLIDING

Hang gliding (above) provides a great thrill and a chance to view spectacular mountain scenery from the air. The hang gliders are carried along by thermals, the warm air currents that rise up mountainsides.

Mount Rushmore
The faces of four American presidents were carved out of a cliff called Mount Rushmore in South Dakota. Shown below, from left to right, are George Washington, Thomas Jefferson, Theodore Roosevelt, and Abraham Lincoln. The head of Washington is 59 feet (18 m) high.

High places have always been sacred to ancient beliefs. To the ancient Greeks, Mount Olympus, the highest mountain in Greece, was the home of their gods. Even in today's world, mountains hold a fascination and mystery that is passed down from generation to generation through stories, myths, and legends.

FAMOUS

MOUNT ARARAT

Mount Ararat (below, left) has the highest summit in Turkey. It has two peaks 7 miles (11 km) apart, joined by a ridge. Great Ararat is 16,945 feet (5,165 m) high; Little Ararat, to the southeast, is 12,782 ft (3,896 m). Traditionally, Mount Ararat has been held by Jews and Christians as the place where Noah's Ark came to rest at the end of the Flood. The *Bible* tells the story of Noah in the Book of Genesis. The mountains of Great and Little Ararat are cone-shaped volcanoes that formed at the border of two colliding tectonic plates. Movement of the plates results in earthquakes and occasional volcanic eruptions in eastern Turkey.

ON CLOSER INSPECTION
– Sacred Uluru

Uluru (formerly Ayer's Rock), in Australia, is a sacred place to the Aboriginal people. It is a mass of sandstone 1,115 feet (340 m) high and nearly 5.6 miles (9 km) around the base that formed more than 450 million years ago.

MOUNTAINS

Fujiyama
Japan's volcanoes are all sacred. The most famous and the highest is Mount Fuji (below).

DEVIL'S TOWER

Devil's Tower is a volcanic plug, the solidified remains of the rock that once formed the core of a volcano, but is now exposed by erosion. The Wyoming Indians say the tower raised itself out of the ground to save seven small girls who were being chased by a bear. They say the vertical markings that formed as the lava cooled and shrank were made by the bear's claws.

Called Fujiyama in Japanese, it is a symbol of purity and eternity to the Japanese. Its name was given by the aboriginal Ainu people after their fire goddess, Fuchi. Every year pilgrims climb Fujiyama, leaving offerings in the temples that line their ascent.

A coral reef encircles a tranquil lagoon around Bora Bora's volcano.

Mount Erebus is the only active volcano in Antarctica. It rises to a height of 13,202 feet (4,024 m). It has a crater lake of bubbling lava. Minor cones eject "bombs" of lava through the air several times a day. Jets of steam can be seen from a distance coming from the crater.

Steam rises from the crater of Mount Erebus over Ross Island in McMurdo Sound, Antarctica.

AMAZING MOUNTAIN FACTS

The island of Surtsey is a volcano that lies south of Iceland. It broke above sea level in 1963 and was named Surtsey after an ancient Icelandic god of fire. It has continued to grow larger since then and has now become home to many plants, insects, and birds.

The Salto Angel (Angel Falls) on the Carrao River in Venezuela is the tallest waterfall in the world. The water falls 3,212 feet (979 m) in total. The longest single drop is 2,648 feet (807 m).

Mauna Kea in Hawaii is the tallest mountain in the world, from its base to its summit. Although only 13,796 feet (4,205 m) above sea level, Mauna Kea rises more than 30,000 feet (10,000 m) from the seafloor.

Mount Everest is the highest mountain on land. It is one of the mountains that make up the Himalayas and is found on the frontiers of Nepal and Tibet. It is 29,028 feet (8,848 m) high. The Himalayas are still rising.

The highest eruption from a geyser was recorded in 1903. The Waimangu geyser in New Zealand shot water to a height of 1,500 feet (457 m). That is higher than the Sears Tower in Chicago. One of its explosive eruptions killed four people in 1903. The geyser is no longer active. It hasn't erupted since 1904.

Mount Everest was named after Sir George Everest (1790–1866), a British surveyor general in India.

Active A volcano that is erupting or showing signs of future eruption.

Altitude The vertical distance measured from sea level.

Atoll A ring-shaped coral island surrounding a shallow body of water, or lagoon.

Avalanche A fall of snow, rock, or ice down a mountainside.

Climate The average weather of an area over a long period of time.

Crater The hollow at the top of a volcano.

Crust The outer solid layer of the earth. There are two types of crust: the thinner, heavier oceanic crust and the thicker, lighter continental crust.

Dormant A volcano that is not erupting, but may erupt again.

Earthquake A shaking or shuddering of the ground due to movements of the earth's crust along a fault.

Erosion The removal of material such as soil or rock fragments by wind, water, ice, and gravity.

Extinct A volcano that has not erupted for thousands of years and is not expected to again.

Fault A crack or break in rock along which movement has taken place.

Fold A bend in layers of rock caused by pressure.

Glacier A mass of ice that moves downhill under its own weight as a result of gravity.

Graben The sunken block between two faults producing a valley called a rift valley.

Horst The raised area between two faults.

Hydroelectricity Electricity produced using the energy from flowing water.

Hydrothermal power Power produced using heated water. Water that is warmed as a result of underground heat, such as that from volcanic activity, is termed geothermal.

Lava Molten rock erupted from volcanoes.

Magma Hot molten rock beneath the earth's surface.

GLOSSARY

Mountain chain Mountain ranges along a line or several parallel lines.

Mountain range A line of mountain ridges.

Mountain system A grouping of mountain chains, mountain ranges, and hundreds of peaks.

Plate tectonics A theory suggesting the earth's outer layers are made of solid sections called plates that move relative to one another.

Snow line The height on a mountain or slope above which snow is permanent and does not melt in the summer.

Sonar System used to locate things underwater by picking up the reflections, or echoes, of short bursts of sound from obstacles in their path.

Volcano A crack in the earth's crust from which lava, gases, steam, and ash are forced out onto the surface.

Weathering The breaking down of rock by exposure to the atmosphere.

INDEX